Integrity

Ethics in the Workplace

Beckie Steele and Elaine Voci

Augsburg Fortress, Minneapolis

Contents

INTERSECTIONS
Small Group Series

Integrity
Ethics in the Workplace

Developed in cooperation with the Division for Congregational Ministries

George S. Johnson, series introduction
Carol A.V.R. Throntveit and Jill Carroll Lafferty, editors
The Wells Group, series design
Cover: Images copyright © 1998 PhotoDisc, Inc.

Scripture quotations are from New Revised Standard Version Bible, copyright 1989 Division of Christian Education of the National Council of the Churches of Christ in the United States of America. Used by permission.

Copyright © 1999 Augsburg Fortress
All rights reserved. May not be reproduced.
ISBN 0-8066-3879-6
Manufactured in U.S.A.

1 2 3 4 5 6 7 8 9 0 1 2 3 4 5 6 7 8 9

Introduction

Making ethical choices

Are ethics still relevant in today's world of "spin," where unethical actions can be made to seem "not so bad" or even acceptable, given today's standards of behavior? Do we really expect the same things from ourselves, coworkers, bosses, and employees that our parents expected when they worked? How many of us are prepared to accept the consequences of being a whistle-blower? How many of us would sacrifice a paycheck for the inner peace and satisfaction that comes from righting a wrong or bringing justice to bear? What are we teaching our children by our own examples? What does the Bible say about making ethical decisions?

A case that made headlines concerns a scientist who worked in the tobacco industry and was coerced into signing off on research papers falsely showing that tobacco had no known addictive properties. After three years of struggling with his conscience, he finally came forward and revealed what he knew to government officials. The stormy period that followed resulted in his wife and children leaving him, death threats against him and his family, the initial loss of his job and benefits, the loss of his home, and a smear campaign meant to destroy his reputation and standing in the professional community of which he had been a member for more than 20 years.

Although this man was later able to regain some elements of his former life, and was vindicated by testimony given in Congressional hearings, the personal price he paid never can be fully compensated.

This event reads like a modern cautionary tale for all of us as we contemplate how to behave in the workplace. No doubt you have pondered the "what ifs" of numerous circumstances that have presented challenges to you in your daily work life. It is a common dilemma in modern life that is especially difficult for those who try to live out their Christian principles—to live as Christ would have us live.

The purpose of this study

This small-group study provides an opportunity for you to gather with other Christians who are seriously considering how to put their beliefs into practice. In this study, you will:

- define ethics, exploring the difference between popular and Christian ethics.

- begin to identify or clarify your own Christian ethics.

- examine practical models for making ethical decisions.

- explore ways to live out Christian ethics in the workplace.

- find support as you wrestle with these issues of faith together.

SMALL GROUP SERIES

Welcome into the family of those who are part of small groups! Intersections Small Group Series will help you and other members of your group build relationships and discover ways to connect the Christian faith with your everyday life.

This book is prepared for those who want to make a difference in this world, who want to grow in their Christian faith, as well as for those who are beginning to explore the Christian faith. The information in this introduction to the Intersections small-group experience can help your group make the most out of your time together.

Biblical encouragement

Do not be conformed to this world, but be transformed by the renewing of your minds, so that you may discern what is the will of God—what is good and acceptable and perfect. Romans 12:2

Small groups provide an atmosphere where the Holy Spirit can transform lives. As you share your life stories and learn together, God's Spirit can work to enlighten and direct you.

Strength is provided to face the pressures to conform to forces and influences that are opposed to what is "good and acceptable and perfect." To "be transformed" is an ongoing experience of God's grace as we take up the cross and follow Jesus. Changed lives happen as we live in community with one another. Small groups encourage such change and growth.

What is a small group?

A number of definitions and descriptions of the small-group ministry experience exist throughout the church. Roberta Hestenes, a Presbyterian pastor and author, defines a small group as an intentional face-to-face gathering of three to twelve people who meet regularly with the common purpose of discovering and growing in the possibilities of the abundant life.

Whatever definition you use, the following characteristics are important.

Small—Seven to ten people is ideal so that everyone can be heard and no one's voice is lost. More than twelve members makes genuine caring difficult.

Intentional—Commitment to the group is a high priority.

Personal—Sharing experiences and insights is more important than mastering content.

Conversational—Leaders that facilitate conversation, rather than teach, are the key to encouraging participation.

Friendly—Having a warm, accepting, nonjudgmental atmosphere is essential.

Christ-centered—The small-group experience is biblically based, related to the real world, and founded on Christ.

Features of Intersections Small Group Series

A small-group model

A number of small-group ministry models exist. Most models include three types of small groups:

- *Discipleship groups*—where people gather to grow in Christian faith and life;

- *Support and recovery group*s—which focus on special interests, concerns, or needs; and

- *Ministry groups*—which have a task-oriented focus.

Intersections Small Group Series offers material for all of these.

For discipleship groups, this series offers a variety of courses with Bible study at the center. What makes a discipleship group different from traditional group Bible studies? In discipleship groups, members bring their life experience to the exploration of the biblical material.

For support and recovery groups, Intersections Small Group Series offers topical material to assist group members in dealing with issues related to their common experience, hurt, or interest. An extra section of facilitator helps in the back of the book will assist leaders of support and recovery groups to anticipate and prepare for special circumstances and needs that may arise as group members explore a topic.

Ministry groups can benefit from an environment that includes prayer, biblical reflection, and relationship building, in addition to their task focus.

Four essentials

Prayer, personal sharing, biblical reflection, and a group ministry task are part of each time you gather. These are all important for Christian community to be experienced. Each of the six chapter themes in each book includes:

- short prayers to open and close your time together.

- carefully worded questions to make personal sharing safe, nonthreatening, and voluntary.

- a biblical base from which to understand and discover the power and grace of God. God's Word is the compass that keeps the group on course.

- a group ministry task to encourage both individuals and the group as a whole to find ways to put faith into action.

Flexibility

Each book contains six chapter themes that may be covered in six sessions or easily extended for groups that meet for a longer period of time. Each chapter theme is organized around two to three main topics with supplemental material to make it easily adaptable to your small group's needs. You need not use all the material. Most themes will work well for 1½- to 2-hour sessions, but a variety of scheduling options is possible.

Bible-based

Each of the six chapter themes in the book includes one or more Bible texts printed in its entirety from the New Revised Standard Version of the Bible. This makes it easy for all group members to read and learn from the same text. Participants will be encouraged through questions, with exercises, and by other group members to address biblical texts in the context of their own lives.

User-friendly

The material is prepared in such a way that it is easy to follow, practical, and does not require a professional to lead it. Designating one to be the facilitator to guide the group is important, but there is no requirement for this person to be theologically trained or an expert in the course topic. Many times options are given so that no one will feel forced into any set way of responding.

Group goals and process

1. Creating a group covenant or contract for your time together will be important. During your first meeting, discuss these important characteristics of all small groups and decide how your group will handle them.

Confidentiality—Agreeing that sensitive issues that are shared remain in the group.

Regular attendance—Agreeing to make meetings a top priority.

Nonjudgmental behavior—Agreeing to confess one's own shortcomings, if appropriate, not those of others, and not giving advice unless asked for it.

Prayer and support—Being sensitive to one another, listening, becoming a caring community.

Accountability—Being responsible to each other and open to change.

Items in your covenant should be agreed upon by all members. Add to the group covenant as you go along. Space to record key aspects is included in the back of this book. See page 53.

2. Everyone is responsible for the success of the group, but do arrange to have one facilitator who can guide the group process each time you meet.

The facilitator is not a teacher or healer. Teaching, learning, and healing happen from the group experience. The facilitator is more of a shepherd who leads the flock to where they can feed and drink and feel safe.

Remember, an important goal is to experience genuine love and community in a Christ-centered atmosphere. To help make this happen, the facilitator encourages active listening and honest sharing. This person allows the material to facilitate opportunities for self-awareness and interaction with others.

Leadership is shared in a healthy group, but the facilitator is the one designated to set the pace, keep the group focused, and enable the members to support and care for each other.

People need to sense trust and freedom as the group develops; therefore, avoid "shoulds" or "musts" in your group.

3. Taking on a group ministry task can help members of your group balance personal growth with service to others.

In your first session, identify ways your group can offer help to others within the congregation or in your surrounding community. Take time at each meeting to do or arrange for that ministry task. Many times it is in the doing that we discover what we believe or how God is working in our lives.

4. Starting or continuing a personal action plan offers a way to address personal needs that you become aware of in your small-group experience.

For example, you might want to spend more time in conversation with a friend or spouse. Your action plan might state, "I plan to visit with Terry two times before our next small-group meeting."

If you decide to pursue a personal action plan, consider sharing it with your small group. Your group can be helpful in at least three ways: by giving support; helping to define the plan in realistic, measurable ways; and offering a source to whom you can be accountable.

5. Prayer is part of small-group fellowship. There is great power in group prayer, but not everyone feels free to offer spontaneous prayer. That's okay.

Learning to pray aloud takes time and practice. If you feel uncomfortable, start with simple and short prayers. And remember to pray for other members between sessions.

Use page 53 in the back of this book to note prayer requests made by group members.

6. Consider using a journal to help reflect on your experiences and insights between meeting times.

Writing about feelings, ideas, and questions can be one way to express yourself; plus it helps you remember what so often gets lost with time.

The "Daily Walk" component includes material that can get your journaling started. This, of course, is up to you and need not be done on any regular schedule. Even doing it once a week can be time well spent.

How to use this book

The material provided for each session is organized around some key components. If you are the facilitator for your small group, be sure to read this section carefully.

The facilitator's role is to establish a hospitable atmosphere and set a tone that encourages participants to share, reflect, and listen to each other. Some important practical things can help make this happen.

- Whenever possible meet in homes. Be sure to provide clear directions about how to get there.
- Use name tags for several sessions.
- Place the chairs in a circle and close enough for everyone to hear and feel connected.
- Be sure everyone has access to a book; preparation will pay off.
- Have Bibles available and encourage participants to bring their own.

Welcoming

The small-group setting is meant to be a place where all can be blessed by the strength, support, and comfort of others. It is a chance to share insights and experiences that are part of one's uniquely individual spiritual journey and to discover Christ's intentions for our journey as a Christian people living together as the body of Christ.

This course is titled *Integrity: Ethics in the Workplace*. Group discussions of such issues can be difficult, as personal experiences and viewpoints may hinder one's ability to step back and take a fresh look. For that reason it is very important that participants feel at home, welcomed, and valued in the group.

To help create a welcoming place, provide a meeting place that both allows for privacy and creates a retreat atmosphere. A comfortable room in the church or a participant's home would work well. Try to minimize distractions by closing doors and turning off the telephone ringer. Welcome group members personally as they arrive. It will also help to provide name tags so that everyone is on equal footing and new-comers feel at home.

Focus

Each of the six chapter themes in this book has a brief focus statement. Read it aloud. It will give everyone a sense of the direction for each session and provide some boundaries so that people will not feel lost or frustrated trying to cover everything. The focus also connects the theme to the course topic.

Community building

This opening activity is crucial to a re-laxed, friendly atmosphere. It will prepare the ground for gradual group development. Two "Community Building" options are provided under each theme. With the facilitator giving his or her response to the questions first, others are free to follow.

One purpose for this section is to allow everyone to participate as he or she re-sponds to nonthreatening questions. The activity serves as a check-in time when participants are invited to share how things are going or what is new.

Make this time light and fun; remember, humor is a welcome gift. Use fifteen to twenty minutes for this activity in your first few sessions.

During your first meeting, encourage group members to write down names and phone numbers (when appropriate) of the other members, so people can keep in touch. Use page 52 for this purpose.

Discovery

This component focuses on exploring the theme for your time together, using material that is read and questions and exercises that encourage sharing of personal insights and experiences.

Reading material includes a Bible text with supplemental passages and commentary written by the topic writer. Have volunteers read the Bible texts aloud. The main passage to be used is printed so that everyone operates from a common translation and sees the text.

"A Further Look" is included in some places to give you additional study material if time permits. Use it to explore related passages and questions. Be sure to have extra Bibles handy.

Questions and exercises related to the theme will invite personal sharing and storytelling. Keep in mind that as you listen to each other's stories, you are inspired to live more fully in the grace and will of God. Such exchanges make Christianity relevant and transformation more likely to happen. Caring relationships are key to clarifying one's beliefs. Sharing personal experiences and insights is what makes the small group spiritually satisfying.

Most people are open to sharing their life stories, especially if they're given permission to do so and they know someone will actively listen. Starting with the facilitator's response usually works best. On some occasions you may want to break the group into units of three or four persons to explore certain questions. When you reconvene, relate your experience to the whole group. The phrase "explore and relate," which appears occasionally in the margin, refers to this recommendation. If your group includes couples, encourage them to separate for this smaller group activity. Appoint someone to start the discussion.

Wrap-up

Plan your schedule so that there will be enough time for wrapping up. This time can include work on your group ministry task, review of key discoveries during your time together, identifying personal and prayer concerns, closing prayers, and the Lord's Prayer.

The facilitator can help the group identify and plan its ministry task. Introduce the idea and decide on your group ministry task in the first session. Tasks need not be grandiose. Activities might include:

- Ministry in your community, such as adopting a food shelf, clothes closet, or homeless shelter; sponsoring equipment, food, or clothing drives; or sending members to staff the shelter.

- Ministry to members of the congregation, such as writing notes to those who are ill or bereaved.

- Congregational tasks where volunteers are always needed, such as serving refreshments during the fellowship time after worship, stuffing envelopes for a church mailing, or taking responsibility for altar preparations for one month.

Depending upon the task, you can use part of each meeting time to carry out or plan the task.

In the "Wrap-up," allow time for people to share insights and encouragement and to voice special prayer requests. Just to mention someone who needs prayer is a form of prayer. The "Wrap-up" time may include a brief worship experience with candles, prayers, and singing. You might form a circle and hold hands. Silence can be effective. If you use the Lord's Prayer in your group, select the version that is known in your setting. There is space on page 54 to record the version your group uses. Another closing prayer is also printed on page 54. Before you go, ask members to pray for one another during the week. Remember also any special concerns or prayer requests.

Daily walk

Seven Bible readings and a verse, thought, and prayer for the journey related to the material just discussed are provided for those who want to keep the theme before them between sessions. These brief readings may be used for devotional time. Some group members may want to memorize selected passages. The Bible readings also can be used for supplemental study by the group if needed. Prayer for other group members also can be part of this time of personal reflection.

A word of encouragement

No material is ever complete or perfect for every situation or group. Creativity and imagination will be important gifts for the facilitator to bring to each theme. Keep in mind that it is in community that we are challenged to grow in Jesus Christ. Together we become what we could not become alone. It is God's plan that it be so.

For additional resources and ideas see *Starting Small Groups—and Keeping Them Going* (Minneapolis: Augsburg Fortress, 1995).

1 Christian Ethics

As Christians, our ethics are informed primarily by God's Word and Christ's teaching and example.

Community building

Share your name, the work you do, and why you have chosen to be a part of this study group. Think about your response, and be yourself. You can choose to be brief, detailed, humorous, or serious.

Role models

Read aloud, then ask group members to form pairs, preferably with someone they don't know well at this point.

Role models are people who inspire and influence our personal behavior and beliefs. A significant role model for many people was Mother Teresa. Thousands of people's lives were inspired and influenced by her caring concern for others. Mother Teresa had *integrity*—in other words, she not only declared her beliefs, she lived them.

Option

Silently reflect on the role models you have in your life now. After a few minutes, share your thoughts with a partner. Together, discuss whether role models are still important to us as adults.

Role models don't have to be famous, however. As you grew up there may have been several people who had great impact on you: family members, pastors, community volunteers, teachers, mentors, friends, or others. Talk together with your partner about those who have been role models to you and how they influenced your life.

Opening prayer

Gracious God, we thank you for giving us your word and Christ's example to guide us as we seek to live and work with integrity. Amen

Ethics

The following phrases from the definition of *ethics* in *Webster's Ninth New Collegiate Dictionary* summarize the understanding we will use in discussing ethics in this small-group study:

the discipline dealing with what is good and bad and with moral duty and obligation; a set of moral principles or values; a theory or system of moral values; the principles of conduct governing an individual or a group.

Below are examples of how several individuals have captured their understanding of ethics.

What you do when no one else is looking!

A personal discipline.

A choice between right or wrong.

Laws not to be broken.

A system of moral values.

The triumph of forgiveness over sin.

■ In groups of three or four, discuss these definitions and how they do or do not fit the *Webster's* definition, which we will use.

■ Reconvene as a large group and allow each small group to share comments regarding its discussion.

Why be ethical?

Part of the work of every country is to deal with the moral questions that face it. Today, issues such as abortion, capital punishment, involvement in the policies and behavior of other countries, environmental degradation, and any number of public scandals are a few of the issues sparking moral debate. This public debate is undergirded by the ethical fiber of our society: the personal ethical decisions made by all of us individually in our daily lives. In other words, in a society where the citizens elect their officials and can use their votes to affect public policy, the ethics of the majority of citizens is reflected in the ethics of that society.

Consider: A clerk gives you back three dollars more than you should receive. Do you call it to the clerk's attention and return it, or put it in your purse or pocket and walk away? On what does your decision rest? The amount of the mistake? Whether you found the clerk friendly or attractive and felt he or she "deserved" to have the money back? Maybe it depends on your own need for money.

If you receive someone else's interoffice mail, do you read it before sending it on? Again—how do you decide? Do you read it only if it came from a certain person or office? If you thought it related to something you also are working on or that involves you? Or, is your respect for privacy such that you would never read it?

You may be thinking that these are small matters with little relevance to the ethical fiber of our society as a whole. And, taken one at a time, such things may be of little immediate consequence except to you and the people directly involved. But add up these and countless other individual choices and collectively they form the base that determines the character of our society, including our workplaces.

- Share some examples of when you have felt or witnessed the effect of the personal ethics of the majority.

Christian ethics

Have Bibles available so the complete text of Exodus 20:1-17 can be read aloud for a broader appreciation of the commandments. Then discuss the questions in this section.

Decisions aren't made in a void. And so, the decision-making process and the moral base informing our decisions are vital components in personal ethics.

As Christians, we do not always agree on moral issues and values. What we can agree on is that we look first to God's Word and Christ's example to inform our morals and values. For purposes of our discussion, that is what we will mean when we use the phrase *Christian ethics*—ethics that are based on and informed by God's Word and Christ's teachings and example.

One of the biblical starting points or set of principles most Christians would look to in ethical decision making is the Ten Commandments.

- Read together the following condensed version of Exodus 20:1-17, or read the full text in your Bibles:

  You shall have no other gods before me. You shall not make wrongful use of the name of the Lord. Remember the Sabbath day, and keep it holy. Honor your father and your mother. You shall not murder. You shall not commit adultery. You shall not steal. You shall not bear false witness against your neighbor. You shall not covet.

One of a child's first exposures to the Christian concept of right and wrong is often a study in Sunday school of the Ten Commandments, which you have just read. The commandments are central to our Christian faith. They instruct us in the way in which we are to live our lives so that we are in right relationship with each other and with God. They are not just Old Testament law to be discarded, as Christ's own words and behavior very often reflect these same teachings. Reflect on the Ten Commandments by discussing these questions:

- How, if at all, do you see the Ten Commandments reflected in the ethical systems of non-Christians today?

- Which commandment or commandments do you witness being broken most often in our society? How? Why?

- Why do you think the first commandment, "You shall have no other gods before me," is considered to be foundational to all the others?

Have members complete this activity individually and then invite sharing of ideas.

Consider this

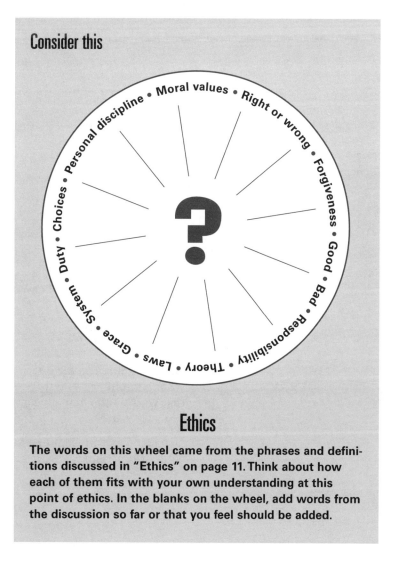

Personal discipline • Moral values • Right or wrong • Forgiveness • Good • Bad • Responsibility • Theory • Laws • Grace • System • Duty • Choices

Ethics

The words on this wheel came from the phrases and definitions discussed in "Ethics" on page 11. Think about how each of them fits with your own understanding at this point of ethics. In the blanks on the wheel, add words from the discussion so far or that you feel should be added.

A further look

Consider Jesus' words related in Matthew and Mark. Read Matthew 5:17-19 and Mark 12:28-31.

■ How do these passages help you know where to start when needing to make an ethical decision?

Discovery

Integrity

Explore and relate.

The name of this course is *Integrity: Ethics in the Workplace. Webster's Ninth New Collegiate Dictionary* defines *integrity* as "an unimpaired condition" or "firm adherence to a code of . . . values." Some might say integrity is putting your money where your mouth is! I may proclaim my ethics and even deeply believe in the morals and values on which they are based, but I cannot claim integrity until I act on those morals and values. Without integrity, then, ethics is nothing more than a mind game.

As Christians, our integrity in living out ethics based on God's Word and Christ's example is a faith response that becomes a reflection of Christ's love within us and a witness to the gospel. To have such integrity relies on a close relationship to God and the support of the Christian community.

■ In groups of three, read each of the following passages, then try to think of a circumstance that could arise in a workplace for which the passage might inform an ethical response.

"Do not judge by appearances, but judge with right judgment" (John 7:24).

"Let justice roll down like waters, and righteousness like an everflowing stream" (Amos 5:24).

"Live in harmony with one another; do not be haughty, but associate with the lowly; do not claim to be wiser than you are" (Romans 12:16).

"Let no evil talk come out of your mouths, but only what is useful for building up, as there is need, so that your words may give grace to those who hear" (Ephesians 4:29).

"Do justice . . . love kindness . . . walk humbly with your God" (Micah 6:8).

Discuss as a group.

A further look

Divide into two groups, assigning each group one of the passages from 1 Peter to read and discuss by responding to the questions.

Read 1 Peter 2:12 and 1 Peter 4:19.

■ How do Peter's words challenge us? How might they comfort us or help us to find the courage to act in difficult situations?

Discovery

Read and discuss. After statements are completed, invite those who wish to share their statements.

The workplace: office, farm, school, home, hospital, church, factory—the list is endless. In many of those workplaces today employees must sign and agree to adhere to a written set of business ethics. These policies help to define a company's values and aim to assure that those values are maintained. If your workplace has a business ethics policy, share some of what the policy demands and how employees react to it. If your workplace doesn't have one, describe situations you know of for which having a policy in place would have been helpful.

■ Take a few minutes now to write a one- or two-sentence statement of business ethics that you would be proud to have represent you in your work.

Group goals

Discuss these issues and record ideas on the "Group Commitments" page in the appendix.

What are your goals for the study of this topic? Use the list below or create your own. Try to agree on two or three group goals.

    a. learn how to make ethical decisions in my daily work life that reflect God's Word and Christ's example

    b. explore ways to live out my Christian ethics with integrity

    c. better understand God's purpose for my life

    d. study God's Word and grow closer to God

    e. find and give support through prayer and dialogue

    g. other

Group commitments

What commitments will you make to one another? Use the suggested categories below as a guide for setting ground rules for your group. See the series introduction (page 6) for information.

    a. confidentiality

    b. regular attendance

    c. nonjudgmental and courteous behavior

    d. openness and participation in discussion

    e. prayer and reflection

    f. support during and between sessions

    g. personal accountability

Group ministry task

Consider together how you as a group can help others in your church and community. Look at pages 6 and 9 of this book and *Starting Small Groups—and Keeping Them Going*, Training Handout 20A, for suggestions.

Wrap-up

See page 9 in the intro-
duction for a description
of "Wrap-up."

Before you go, take time for the following:

- Group ministry task

- Review

Ongoing prayer requests
can be listed on page
53. See page 54 for sug-
gested closing prayers.

- Personal concerns and prayer concerns

- Closing prayers

Daily walk

Bible Readings

Day 1
Exodus 20:4-6

Day 2
Exodus 20:7

Day 3
Exodus 20:8-11

Day 4
Exodus 20:12

Day 5
Exodus 20:13-16

Day 6
Exodus 20:17

Day 7
Exodus 20:18-20

Verse for the journey

"I am the LORD your God . . . you shall have no other gods before me" (Exodus 20:2-3).

Thought for the journey

I can proclaim my Christian ethics, but I will not know integrity until those ethics are lived.

Prayer for the journey

God of Wisdom, make me keenly aware of ethical choices I
make each day, and help me act with courage. In Jesus' name,
Amen

2 Making Ethical Decisions

Identifying ethical issues and exploring Christian approaches to their resolution helps us to move from declaration to action.

Community building

Invite members to respond to one of these.

- Name a person at your workplace who often makes your day or inspires you and say how.

- Name something about your place of employment that you value highly and explain why.

- Name one aspect of your job that you truly enjoy and that encourages you to stay.

Option

Share a little of how you go about making major decisions. Do you carefully weigh options? Go with your instincts? Seek advice? Other?

Check-in

- Sitting in groups of two to three, share with one another a high point and a low point from your week. When all have shared, pray together the opening prayer.

Opening prayer

Gracious God, guide us in our journey toward making ethical decisions that reflect and witness to the love that you have given us. Amen

Decisions

Before reading and discussing, review the definition of *ethics* found on page 11 and *Christian ethics* on page 12.

After reading each of the following situations, work together to identify:

    a. what further information is needed to make a decision.

    b. who will be affected and how by each course of action.

    c. possible dangers from making a judgment too quickly or too slowly.

Refer back to the Ten Commandments and the other Bible passages discussed in chapter 1 or other Bible passages you know to inform your decisions.

Am I reflecting Christian ethics if:

    a. I serve larger portions of food to some people than to others?

    b. I report a coworker's personality problem to my boss?

    c. I help friends and family save money by having them call me at work using the company's toll-free long distance phone number?

    d. I refuse to comply with a company decision?

    e. I refuse to lend farm equipment to a neighbor?

    f. I use my knowledge, skills, or position to control others?

    g. I ignore language or behavior that is degrading to others?

    h. I do nothing, even though I know that several doctors with whom I volunteer at a free clinic appear to rush through patient examinations, often seeing twice as many in an hour as they do in their private practices?

Gut reactions

Read and complete activity. Consider discussing the first two group discussion questions by holding mini-debates on the issues.

Most of us have an internal sense (often called a conscience) that helps us make decisions and "feel" if our actions are right or wrong. We know when we are unsettled in a situation because we cannot get it off our mind, or we may have a queasy stomach or other physical reaction as we struggle for an answer.

It has been noted by psychologists that our bodies never "lie" and that these internal signals are meant to help us make the right choice and do the right thing according to the values and beliefs that have been cultivated within us.

Working alone, respond to the following by writing your answers on note paper or the margins of your book:

- Describe the internal signals that let you know when you are "off course" from your ethical principles.

- What happens when you take action based on the signals?

- What happens when you try to ignore them?

- Do you consider these signals as communication from God? Explain.

When you've completed your answers, put your paper away and make eye contact with your facilitator to indicate that you are ready to continue.

When everyone is finished, move to a discussion of the following questions, allowing both individual and group response as appropriate.

- If consistently ignored, what happens to one's conscience?

- What is a social conscience?

- How influential is the conscience of the community on one's personal conscience? Not at all influential? Somewhat? Very?

- Using a scale of 1 to 10, with 1 being "very weak" and 10 being "very strong," rank how strong you think the communal conscience is:

    a. in the place where you work.

    | 1 | 2 | 3 | 4 | 5 | 6 | 7 | 8 | 9 | 10 |

    b. in your community.

    | 1 | 2 | 3 | 4 | 5 | 6 | 7 | 8 | 9 | 10 |

    c. in your country.

    | 1 | 2 | 3 | 4 | 5 | 6 | 7 | 8 | 9 | 10 |

Putting it to the test

Read and discuss.

Many programs on ethical decision making provide a list of questions to help people decide the right or wrong of a situation. The following are four key questions to use in considering ethical decisions from a Christian perspective.

1. Will my actions show unconditional love to the others involved in the situation?

2. Are there specific biblical teachings that apply to this situation? If not, how can I apply my knowledge of God's Word and Christ's example to this specific dilemma?

3. What answer does my own conscience tell me will bring me inner peace, even though it also may be painful?

4. What faith example will I provide to my coworkers and my family by the decision I make?

In using this test in regard to Christian ethics, it is essential that we recognize the centrality of Jesus' teachings, the underlying message or value to which he speaks. What do you think is the centrality of Jesus' message on ethics? Reflect on Christ's words in Matthew for ideas.

Matthew 22:35-39

35 . . . one of them . . . asked . . . 36 "Teacher, which commandment in the law is the greatest?" 37 [Jesus] said to him, " 'You shall love the Lord your God with all your heart, and with all your soul, and with all your mind.' 38 This is the greatest and first commandment. 39 And a second is like it: 'You shall love your neighbor as yourself.'"

■ How are the questions listed above reflected in Christ's words? What changes or additions, if any, would you make to the test questions so that they more clearly reflect Christ's message?

A further look

Explore and relate by having one group answer the questions using the Ten Commandments (page 12) as a basis and the other using the test questions from "Putting It to the Test."

Find and read Luke 6:27-36 in your Bible.

Should personal forgiveness and mercy be a part of complying to written business ethics of one's workplace? Consider the following situation:

John sees a coworker who is not authorized to do so slip $100 from the petty cash file. John knows finances are so tight that there are times that this person's family goes without eating. He believes the person will return the money and knows the petty cash account is not monitored closely and the situation is unlikely to be discovered. John, upon his employment, however, signed and agreed to the company's written policy, which states that anyone observing another person breaking company policy or involved in unauthorized activity must report that incident to the human resources department.

■ What ethical issues are at play here? What is the right thing to do? According to what standards?

■ Does the right thing allow John to live out the Christian principles of forgiveness and mercy? Must it?

■ Read Exodus 1:8-22. How is that situation similar to or different from John's dilemma?

Discovery

A different look

Read and discuss.

You've heard it. It's that "tape" playing in your head of a parent or other significant adult saying "don't steal, don't lie, don't hurt others." God's message tape goes a step further and calls us beyond these basic messages to a broader understanding. In such an understanding, the admonition that we should not steal includes more than taking someone's material possessions; it includes the taking away of his or her good name or reputation through defaming or gossiping about him or her. Or, in considering the commandment to not commit adultery, we are pushed to see that it is also a wandering and lustful eye for another that must be subdued. With these and all the messages inherent in the Ten Commandments and Jesus' teachings, we are called to think past the surface parameters. Simply put, God asks us to look at ethics differently than others. Jesus said, "You are the light of the world. . . . Let your light shine before others, so that they may see your good works and give glory to your Father in heaven" (Matthew 5:14, 16).

■ How do Jesus' words provide a model for ethical decision making?

What about this?

Read and discuss.

Loida Nicolas Lewis, CEO of TLC Beatrice International of New York, a multinational business with operations in Europe and Asia, shared in the Sept. 6, 1998, *Parade* magazine these rules for success in business:

Love your neighbor.

Give your customers a quality product.

Be attentive to their needs.

Give back to the community.

Copyright © 1998 Loida Nicolas Lewis. Used by permission.

■ What impact might the living out of such values have on the employees who work for Lewis?

■ To what degree do these rules reflect the biblical teachings we have looked at thus far in our study?

■ Would following these rules assure ethical behavior?

Read aloud, then allow
participants to complete
the activity individually.

Consider this

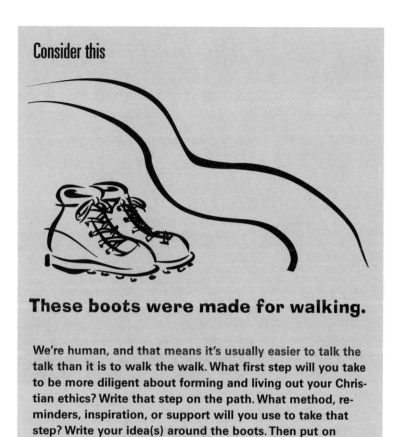

These boots were made for walking.

We're human, and that means it's usually easier to talk the
talk than it is to walk the walk. What first step will you take
to be more diligent about forming and living out your Christian ethics? Write that step on the path. What method, reminders, inspiration, or support will you use to take that
step? Write your idea(s) around the boots. Then put on
those boots and start walking!

A further look

**Read Scripture aloud
and discuss.**

Read James 1:19-21.

■ What does "welcome with meekness" mean to you?

■ What advice do these words give us about ethical decision making? About passing judgment on others or their
actions?

■ How can we more fully recognize and encourage God's
Word within us?

Wrap-up

Before you go, take time for the following:

- Group ministry task

- Review

- Personal concerns and prayer concerns

- Closing prayers

Daily walk

Bible readings

Day 1
Matthew 12:46-50

Day 2
Matthew 13:1-9

Day 3
Matthew 13:24-30

Day 4
Matthew 13:31-33

Day 5
Matthew 13:44-50

Day 6
Matthew 13:54-58

Day 7
Matthew 7:24-28

Verse for the journey

"For where your treasure is, there your heart will be also" (Matthew 6:21).

Thought for the journey

When called to choose, I must first ask how my decision will witness to Christ's love within me.

Prayer for the journey

Dear God, strengthen us as we struggle to define and live the ethical life you would have us live, so that we may witness to your great and gracious love. Amen

3 Communication and Relationships

Focus

The way in which we communicate and handle relationships is an opportunity to live out our Christian ethics.

Community building

■ Complete the following statement:

My favorite communication method in my work is (circle one)

phone   e-mail   written   face-to-face

because _____.

Share your response with others in the group. Share also ideas about how each method can either enhance or impede communication and understanding.

Option

Recall and share the most positive work relationship you have ever had and explain what made it so. Try to describe, too, what was positive about how you communicated and related to each other.

Check-in

■ Share your feelings on how the group is going to this point. Is something missing? What is most helpful? Do some things need more time or less time? When finished, pray together the opening prayer.

Opening prayer

Lord, guide our time together. Help us here and elsewhere to communicate with and relate to others in ways that evidence your love in us. Amen

What about others?

Every day we make decisions about the way in which we communicate with and relate to others. Those choices, whether conscious or not, have an effect on how others view us and the integrity of our Christian ethics, how we make others feel about themselves, how effective we are in our personal and work relationships, and our ability to witness the gospel with others. In this chapter, we will look at a variety of communication and relationship issues to help you think about how some of these issues function in your own workplace. Let's begin with a look at Philippians.

Philippians 2:3-5

3 Do nothing from selfish ambition or conceit, but in humility regard others as better than yourselves. 4 Let each of you look not to your own interests, but to the interests of others. 5 Let the same mind be in you that was in Christ Jesus.

- In what ways does this verse represent typical work environment communications and relationships in your experience? Explain.

- Why would or wouldn't a business choose these verses to be its guiding principles?

- How do you see these principles reflected in your workplace?

Is that what you meant?

Encourage everyone to say the phrases.

Say each of the following phrases first as a question, then as an exclamation, and finally as a sarcasm.

Good job

Isn't that wonderful

You've done it again

Right

Tone of voice is important! Most of us have received a written or verbal communication at some time and misinterpreted—or not been sure how to interpret—a particular comment or phrase. Many things other than words enter in, such as the relationship and trust between those communicating and the perceived (or real) tone or attitude. In fact, none of us is always pleasant and positive. Share experiences you have had in your work environment in which someone's style (including your own) of communication created problems or misunderstanding. (Some words to spark memories: sarcasm, anger, dominating, interrupting, bossy, superior.) What was/is the result? How was/could the issue be handled to the benefit of everyone?

Nonverbal responses

Read aloud and discuss. Invite members to share nonverbal cues familiar to them.

A group of coworkers were on the golf course playing when one of them began to tell a joke using racial stereotyping, then noticed one listener's facial expressions grow solemn and severe. This person was clearly uncomfortable and unapproving of the joke under way. The colleague telling the joke quickly reacted to that listener's facial expression by interrupting the joke with a personal coughing fit that lasted twenty or thirty seconds, and after "recovering" from coughing began a conversation of a different nature. None of the other colleagues asked that the joke begun earlier be finished, and no further references to it were made.

- Why do you think the nonverbal response of the listener was effective?

- Name other nonverbal signals that could be effective in this or other situations.

- Was this type of communication enough in this situation or did someone need to address the offense directly? Why or why not?

Out of the mouths of ...

Read aloud and discuss.

Gossip is idle conversation about other people often based on rumor and may or may not be true. Slander is differentiated from gossip in that it is untrue information being spread with the intent to harm someone's reputation or position.

- What generally motivates gossip in your work environment?

- Is it gossip if information is shared out of concern for the person involved?

- Have you ever witnessed slander in your work environment? What motivated it?

- Is participating in gossip or slander always breaking the commandment "You shall not bear false witness against your neighbor"? Explain.

- Share ideas for handling gossip or slander that would fit with living out one's Christian ethics.

A further look

Read aloud and discuss.

"A gossip goes about telling secrets, but one who is trustworthy in spirit keeps a confidence" (Proverbs 11:13). Carefully consider how you might react the next time a fellow worker wants to pass along some gossip with you. If your goal is to discourage it without sounding preachy or "holier than thou," what responses could you make?

Discovery

Who's the sensitive one?

Have members read silently, then discuss.

A human resource director was visited by an employee complaining of his boss's sometimes gruff and abrupt way of communicating. Overall, the employee was quite satisfied with the boss's manners, professionalism, and decisions, but the occasional lapses into moodiness were upsetting; one never knew what to expect. The human resource manager suggested the employee make a list of the positive and negative qualities his boss possessed in the work environment. After finishing and reviewing the list, she counseled the employee to practice giving the boss the benefit of the doubt. She shared with him a couple of what she called "anyway" guides to working with others:

People are illogical, unreasonable, and self-centered. Love and trust them anyway.

People really need help but may attack you if you do help them. Help people anyway.

The employee left the manager's office with a heightened appreciation of his boss's strengths and a commitment to overlook his occasional bad moods.

- What other "anyway" guides would you add and why?

- Under what circumstances might using "anyway" guides not be a good choice?

- If you were the employee, explain whether or not you would be satisfied with the human resource manager's response?

- Do the "anyway" guides reflect the Ten Commandments and what you know of Christ's teachings and example? Explain.

Acts 2:44-47

44 All who believed were together and had all things in common; 45 they would sell their possessions and goods and distribute the proceeds to all, as any had need. 46 Day by day, as they spent much time together in the temple, they broke bread at home and ate their food with glad and generous hearts, 47 praising God and having the goodwill of all the people. And day by day the Lord added to their number those who were being saved.

Making a list, checking it twice

Have a large sheet of paper or whiteboard on which to make the lists.

Many would say that Christian ethics demand that we live the lifestyle described in the above passage from Acts—sharing equally with all, acting with love and kindness toward each other, and focusing on praising God rather than material wealth or personal position. That is hardly the premise of most work environments. Make a chart with two columns. Label one "Separate" and the other "Unite." In the first column, list all the things that separate people in work environments (for example, education, position, clothing, strength). In the second column, list the things you can think of that unite people (for example, respect, skill-sharing, knowing each other, uniforms).

When you finish, talk about ways to change those things that separate people and encourage those that unite. Remember, not all solutions have to be major. Small steps can result in a journey!

Put yourself in each column. In what ways do you feel you contribute to the first column, whether purposely or not? In what ways do or will you contribute to the second column?

Connecting

Read aloud and discuss.

Kay Gilley writes in *Leading from the Heart*: "To build relationships it is important to know what gets in the way of connection. . . . We must bring our true, whole, authentic self, complete with beliefs, values, and emotions, to others with whom we live and work. We risk being vulnerable; instead of mechanically saying, doing, or feeling what we believe we 'should' say, do, or feel, we honestly share what we are actually feeling" (Newton, Mass.: Butterworth-Heinemann, 1997, page 144).

- What would it be like to work for an organization that espoused these ideas?

- Would you expect people to gossip or speak slanderously of one another in an organization that followed these ideas?

- What is learned by directly addressing our honest emotions that we can't learn by suppressing them?

- What are positive ways one could discover what is getting "in the way of connection"?

- What Christian principles fit with the ideas expressed in the quote?

Consider this

PhotoDisc, Inc. © 1997

- **What does your face say about who you are? What do others see in your face when working with you? Is it pleasant, inviting, and friendly, building people up rather than bringing them down? Does God's love shine through you to be shared with others?**

A further look

Use brainstorming to get ideas flowing. Remind participants to wait until after all ideas are on the board to make comments about the ideas.

Read 2 Timothy 1:3-14 in your Bible.

Stating that we belong to Christ can be a risky business in our modern world. Some, perhaps even we ourselves, are uncomfortable with those who are bold in their declarations of salvation and the gospel. We may have a more negative than positive response to someone asking "I am saved, are you?" In some places religious conversation is limited or not allowed. How, then, can we share the gospel with others?

Wrap-up

Before you go, take time for the following:

- Group ministry task

- Review

- Personal concerns and prayer concerns

- Closing prayers

Daily walk

Bible readings

Day 1
Romans 12:3-8

Day 2
Romans 12:9-13

Day 3
Romans 12:14-19

Day 4
Romans 13:1-7

Day 5
Romans 14:1-4

Day 6
Romans 14:7-12

Day 7
Romans 15:1-6

Verse for the journey

"A soft answer turns away wrath, but a harsh word stirs up anger" (Proverbs 15:1).

Thought for the journey

Striving to live out my Christian ethics in the workplace isn't a duty, it is a faith response.

Prayer for the journey

My God, help us to be creative, diligent, and supportive of each other in our efforts to communicate with and relate to those with whom we work in a way that reflects the gospel. Amen

4 The Real World

Identifying and acknowledging sources that influence our standards of ethical behavior can strengthen us to live and act with integrity.

Community building

Have available three sheets of different colored paper labeled as described.

■ Three sheets of paper will be passed to you, each with one of these labels: "If you want me to do you a favor just offer me _____;" "If I could trade bodies with anyone, it would be _____;" or "The television, movie, or book character I'd most like to change lives with for six months is _____."

When you receive the paper, write your answer on it, then pass it on. Do NOT pass it to a person on either side of you unless everyone else has already had it. When everyone is done, read each sheet aloud.

Without putting too much weight on it, what inklings did you get about societal influences from this humorous look at the kinds of things that motivate or impress people?

Option

In groups of three, share light-hearted stories of times your actions were heavily influenced by society's standards or the media. For example, as a teenager you may have insisted on wearing a popular fashion that you now can't believe you wore because it truly did look as bad on you as your parents said!

Check-in

■ Share a high point and low point from your week. When all have shared, hold hands in a circle and pray: Lord, help us to feel your presence in our times of need and to rejoice in your blessings. Amen

Discovery

Bring several different general interest magazines to this session, enough so that each pair of participants will have one to use.

In pairs, examine the magazine you have been given. What do the title, cover image, and featured articles tell you about who the magazine is for and the values the magazine assumes the reader holds? Page through the magazine. Are a majority of the ads promoting similar products? What are those products and why would someone buy them? Do the models in ads (male and female) have typical bodies, or are almost all the men trim and well-muscled and the women extremely thin and long-legged? Look at the pictures in the magazine. Do they reflect stereotyping of particular groups? Are some groups not included? Why might that be? How would you say this magazine reflects society as a whole? What general values does the magazine promote?

After all pairs have finished, have each one share some of what they learned or noticed with the large group. Then as a large group discuss these questions:

- What difference, if any, does it make what images are used, groups are represented, or ads are prevalent in a magazine you read regularly?

- What four questions would you ask regarding content in deciding whether to subscribe to a magazine to be certain it fits with your values?

I only listen to the music

Be prepared to play a portion of a popular song that has sexually explicit or graphically violent language or to show a short video segment from a current movie that contains a sexually explicit scene or is laden with cursing and swearing.

We've all heard it—maybe even said it! When challenged about the language used in a song, the answer often is "I only listen to the music! The words don't matter." Your group leader has music or a video for you to evaluate. After your listening or viewing, share opinions on the appropriateness of the content for the intended audience. Next, share the evaluation measures you use in making these decisions for yourself.

■ Use a raising of hands to indicate group members' responses to this question: How valid a measure of a person's morals and values is the content of what he or she listens to or views in the media?

Very valid   Moderately valid   Of little validity

Explain your viewpoints with others.

Discuss.

■ Morals and values, such as the Christian principles found in God's Word and Christ's example, inform one's ethics and thus are a vital aspect of ethical decision making. Can one be said then, to be ethical if he or she has no awareness of his or her own morals and values?

Romans 12:1-2

Read text aloud, then allow several minutes for individuals to reflect on their own answers to the questions.

¹ I appeal to you therefore, brothers and sisters, by the mercies of God, to present your bodies as a living sacrifice, holy and acceptable to God, which is your spiritual worship. ² Do not be conformed to this world, but be transformed by the renewing of your minds, so that you may discern what is the will of God—what is good and acceptable and perfect.

Paul is speaking of the difference between being *in* the world—fully involved with life and its issues, but guided by God's will and desires, not society's—or being *of* the world and allowing society's concerns to be the stronger influence in our lives. He speaks, too, of the need for our minds to be continually transformed.

Think about you in your workplace. Would your coworkers or those who do business with you consider you *in* or *of* the world? In answering that, consider these three areas:

    a. things I possess and/or display
    b. language or attitudes displayed in my conversation and treatment of others
    c. the people with whom I surround myself

Discovery

Read aloud and discuss.

Beyond the media

How consciously aware are you of the influence factors such as your economic status, your race, your educational level, the peers you choose, your children's friends and school system, or the policies of the business for which you work, have on how you view others and how they view you? Consider:

One person owns the biggest farm in the county and loves it, but feels there's never enough time for family and friends. The person's closest and newest neighbor is starting over after losing a farm to bankruptcy several years ago. The two farmers are of different races and education levels and are ten years apart in age.

■ What assumptions, both positive and negative, might these farmers make about each other?

■ What difficulties might arise in these two farmers forming a relationship?

■ What support might they offer each other?

■ What would you expect to happen in this circumstance? Does your answer depend on knowing who is of what race, more educated, or younger? Did you wonder if they were male or female? Explain.

Within the workplace

Read and discuss.

Having thought about things that influence our decisions, think now about how the workplace, social ethics, and personal ethics work together. Regulations, policies, or laws can sometimes make living your personal Christian ethics difficult. So can particular circumstances surrounding a situation.

■ Share quandaries you have faced around such issues.

■ Brainstorm how one could most fully live out his or her Christian ethics in the face of those difficulties. Do some thinking beyond the walls of your workplace to a more global perspective that might include using products made by sweatshop labor, using fertilizers that help to produce needed food but that pollutes rivers, and so forth. For each quandary, identify the following:

   a. Why do I need to act?
   b. What are the options?
   c. What are the risks to me? To others?
   d. Which action will give me the greatest sense of integrity?

Consider this

"Love with care, and then do what you will."

St. Augustine

■ **In what ways does this quote fit with living out one's Christian ethics? In what ways does it not?**

A further look

Read and discuss.

Ultimately, it is God who judges our ethical behavior. Jesus said, "[The Lord] will answer them, 'Truly I tell you, just as you did not do it to one of the least of these, you did not do it to me.' And these will go away into eternal punishment, but the righteous into eternal life" (Matthew 25:45-46). For a fuller understanding of judgment read this entire passage: Matthew 25:31-46.

■ What inspiration or insight can you draw from this passage to help you approach ethical decision making from a Christian perspective?

Wrap-up

Before you go, take time for the following:

- Group ministry task

- Review

- Personal concerns and prayer concerns

- Closing prayers

Daily walk

Bible readings

Day 1
John 15:18-19

Day 2
John 18:36-37

Day 3
2 Corinthians 3:12-18

Day 4
2 Corinthians 4:16-18

Day 5
2 Corinthians 6:14-18

Day 6
1 John 2:15-17

Day 7
1 John 5:1-5

Verse for the journey

"Owe no one anything, except to love one another; for the one who loves another has fulfilled the law" (Romans 13:8).

Thought for the journey

If I am not aware of and try to control that which influences me, I may never truly know myself.

Prayer for the journey

O God, help me look for your truth in all of the situations I face each day. Encourage me as I seek to be a living sacrifice to you. Amen

5 Putting It into Practice

Focus

Living out one's Christian ethics is a challenge-filled, ongoing journey.

Community building

Allow time for each person to respond.

■ Consider some of the different roles you play in your work, family, and community life. These may include parent, spouse, manager, customer, referee, advocate, son/daughter, or coach. Select one of your most meaningful memories in one of these roles, such as your team winning a championship or your work being recognized in a special way.

Check-in

Have a sponge ball available.

■ Sit in a circle, and give one person a sponge ball that he or she should toss to another person after sharing a prayer concern (either personal, for another person or group, or for the community or world). After all have been tossed the ball and have responded, pray the opening prayer together.

Option

Think for a moment "outside the box." If you could choose a role to live for just one hour that could greatly influence the ethics of our society, what would that role be? Would you choose to influence a group or an individual? What would you want to say and why?

Opening prayer

Dear Lord, we bring these concerns to you and ask that your love surround those involved and our response to them. Amen

Christian ethics are a faith response that grows out of the gift of love and salvation given to us in Christ. And like faith, it is at once simple and complex. Simple because the Christian ethic seems to boil down to "doing the Christlike thing." Complex because it is not always easy to know what the Christlike thing is. In this chapter, you will explore ideas that can help you wrestle with living in a Christlike way.

Ethics check

Read and discuss.

Kenneth Blanchard and Norman Vincent Peale in their book, *The Power of Ethical Management*, have identified three questions called the "Ethics Check," which they suggest using to resolve ethical dilemmas (New York: William Morrow Company, 1988). The questions are: (1) Is it legal? (2) Is it balanced? (3) How will it make me feel about myself? They also describe the five *p's* for ethical power: purpose, pride, patience, persistence, and perspective. These refer to having a clear sense of purpose, taking pride in one's actions and in building and keeping a good reputation, staying patient and persistent in order to see things through no matter how uncomfortable it gets, and keeping a balanced perspective on the situation and our role in it.

- How effective do you think Blanchard and Peale's questions are as a method for maintaining ethical integrity in your particular work environment?

- What questions, if any, should be added? Explain.

A case in point

Read the case study aloud, then divide into three groups and assign each group one of the suggested ethical guides to use in discussing the case. When all groups finish, have each summarize its discussion for the large group.

Robert, a quiet and seemingly aloof supervisor, was accused of sexual harassment by one of his team. Management confronted Robert with the charge, and assured him an investigation fair to both parties would take place. While his accuser was given great sympathy and support by her fellow employees, Robert increasingly was ostracized. Two women colleagues with whom he always had ridden the subway very soon began taking an earlier train. His secretary stood by him, but finally got so tired of defending herself for doing so that she stopped speaking up.

In the end, as no proof could be found, Robert was given an official warning and told the incident would be recorded in his employee file, but that no further disciplinary action would take place. Within a few months, he had fallen into a deep depression and within a year was demoted for not being able to carry out his work. Soon afterward, Robert left the company.

A year-and-a-half later, Robert's accuser—having had too much to drink—bragged that she had lied about the harassment in revenge for poor performance reviews Robert had given her that she felt had cost her a promotion.

How might each of the following guides to making ethical decisions have made an impact on this case? As you discuss, consider how each may have guided management's actions, Richard's actions, the accuser's actions, the colleagues' actions, and expectations in our society. Consider, too, if and/or how each guide falls short as far as usefulness in the case.

    a. Blanchard and Peale's questions
    b. the golden rule: "Do to others as you would have them do to you" (Luke 6:31)
    c. Jesus' behavior in this passage from Mark

Mark 2:13-17

13 Jesus went out again beside the sea; the whole crowd gathered around him, and he taught them. 14 As he was walking along, he saw Levi son of Alphaeus sitting at the tax booth, and he said to him, "Follow me." And he got up and followed him.

15 And as he sat at dinner in Levi's house, many tax collectors and sinners were also sitting with Jesus and his disciples—for there were many who followed him. 16 When the scribes of the Pharisees saw that he was eating with sinners and tax collectors, they said to his disciples, "Why does he eat with tax collectors and sinners?" 17 When Jesus heard this, he said to them, "Those who are well have no need of a physician, but those who are sick; I have come to call not the righteous but sinners."

Consider this

In both families and work environments, a culture of truth must prevail if the members are to be healthy, develop fully, and be productive. Michael Hammer, coauthor of *Reengineering the Corporation*, said in the July 1994 issue of *Culture of Executive Excellence*, "Don't tell the truth because it is right, tell the truth because it works."

■ Why do you or don't you agree with Hammer's statement?

■ Have you ever regretted telling the truth? Explain.

■ Are there circumstances where you feel Christian ethics would support not telling the truth? Explain.

■ In what ways might the emphasis on being inoffensive in our public speech encourage or discourage speaking the truth?

■ How is truth-telling encouraged or discouraged in your work environment? Your family?

A further look

Read this passage aloud and then discuss as a group.

Read Colossians 3:23-24.

■ Why do or don't you consider what you do as done for the Lord rather than your boss, mate, neighbor, friend, or relative? Is there a difference? (See Matthew 25:45.)

■ Recall a time when your actions were carefully watched by others, which caught you by surprise and perhaps embarrassed you.

Discovery

What is the Christlike thing?

Have a large sheet of paper available to record lists.

List qualities you associate with Jesus or Jesus' actions. Now, read aloud the following texts, taking time after each reading to add to your list words that you would associate with Jesus or Jesus' actions in that text.

John 2:13-19

Luke 11:37-53

Luke 12:49-53

- What additional insights do these texts give you as to what constitutes ethics based on God's Word and Christ's example?

- What circumstances do you know of or can you imagine in the work environment, corporate America, rural environments, or elsewhere where doing the Christlike thing may not bring harmony?

Consider this

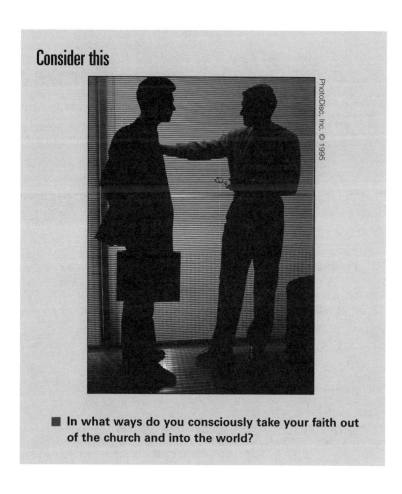

PhotoDisc, Inc. © 1995

- **In what ways do you consciously take your faith out of the church and into the world?**

A further look

Read Mark 9:42-50.

- What is the difference, if any, between what Jesus is warning against in this text and being a poor example or neglecting to be mindful of Christlike behavior?

Wrap-up

Before you go, take time for the following:

- Group ministry task

- Review

- Personal concerns and prayer concerns

- Closing prayers

Daily walk

Bible readings

Day 1
Matthew 4:1-11

Day 2
Matthew 4:18-22

Day 3
Matthew 5:13-16

Day 4
Matthew 5:17-20

Day 5
Matthew 5:21-26

Day 6
Matthew 5:27-30

Day 7
Matthew 5:43-48

Verse for the journey

"Do not worry . . . for the Holy Spirit will teach you at that very hour what you ought to say" (Luke 12:11-12).

Thought for the journey

The only gospel some people will read is my daily example.

Prayer for the journey

God, help us to be aware of our lives as your servants here on earth and to do our task with boldness and humility. Amen

6 My Choices and the Family of God

It is a Christian's responsibility to realize that none of us lives in a vacuum and that all that we do has an effect on others.

Community building

Option

Many of us are willing to take responsibility for our own decisions, but unless it's family or a close friend, we don't feel comfortable getting involved with the decisions of others—even when we have serious concerns about the outcomes of those decisions.

Share a time when you or someone you know had serious concerns about the outcome or effect of someone's decision, but didn't speak up. What reasons cause people to not speak up? What do you think our responsibility for others should be in situations like this?

■ Share the modern communication method you most value and tell why. After hearing from all, discuss how modern communication has changed the world in your lifetime.

Check-in

■ Share how things are going in general with you and those you love. When all have finished, pray together the opening prayer.

Opening prayer

O God, make us mindful of how our action or inaction affects the family of God, and give us the insight, sensitivity, and courage we need to care for each other and the world in which we live. Amen

As in all other aspects of our lives, what we do as our life's work and how we do it has an effect on others. Take for example the farmer who makes a choice between using chemical fertilizers that result in a greater crop yield or using strictly organic methods. Several questions could surround this choice: What is the impact of either choice and on whom? Should the resultant crops of either method be gathered by migrant workers earning little money, but who would otherwise have no employment? When selling fresh fruits and vegetables to restaurants or grocery stores, should they be informed about issues like fertilizers or migrant workers? How much information should go to consumers about the choices that resulted in the food they will eat?

Such questions illustrate how things filter down, and that these are not simple issues. It is impossible to fully live out one's Christian ethics, however, if such issues are simply ignored. And so, in this chapter, we will consider how workplace decisions affect the community, the country, and the world in which we live.

The effect on me

Read and discuss with group members.

Today, technology allows us to rapidly communicate, conduct business transactions, and instantly be made aware of events happening almost anywhere in the world. This has resulted in a greater awareness of our global interdependence. Which of these have had the most impact or caused the greatest concern to you and why?

a. the nuclear test treaty being ignored or broken
b. collapsing economies causing devaluation of your investments
c. the price of heating oil or automobile gasoline jumping in the United States due to an overseas coup or civil uprising in the Middle East
d. the passing of a proposition depriving nondocumented immigrants' children of government-sponsored health care and education
e. inexpensive clothing, household goods, or books being made available at the expense of human rights in other countries

Romans 12:9-18

9 Let love be genuine; hate what is evil, hold fast to what is good; 10 love one another with mutual affection; outdo one another in showing honor. 11 Do not lag in zeal, be ardent in spirit, serve the Lord. 12 Rejoice in hope, be patient in suffering, persevere in prayer. . . .

14 Bless those who persecute you; . . . Rejoice with those who rejoice, weep with those who weep. 16 Live in harmony with one another; do not be haughty. . . . 17 Do not repay anyone evil for evil, but take thought for what is noble in the sight of all. 18 If it is possible, so far as it depends on you, live peaceably with all.

Hold fast

Read aloud, then list on a large sheet of paper the ground rules the group decides upon.

Most of us have been in the midst of a heated discussion. People who are normally calm, respectful, and caring find themselves treating each other in hurtful, disdainful ways. At the base of such behavior are passionate personal feelings for subjects or causes about which we feel there is no compromise. Yet, it is often those subjects or causes that most desperately need respectful and caring consideration. As you work through some of the exercises in this chapter, you may find yourself or others experiencing strong reactions to some of the case studies. Such reactions most often grow out of intense personal experience, and it is helpful to plan ahead, setting ground rules or reminders for discussion. To that end, take time now to list a few ground rules, using the Romans text printed above and the golden rule (Luke 6:31) to guide your thoughts.

Uneasy choices

Read each case aloud, then divide into two groups. Have each group work with one of the cases. When they finish, have the groups share their lists with the large group, taking time for additional comments and discussion as needed or desired.

"You just do what is right." That's the measure many people say is most important in making ethical choices. But how easy is that? Consider the cases below. In doing so, make a list of factors you would use to make a decision, being sure to consider all parties involved.

■ The union has been on strike for six months, and union families are now facing serious financial difficulties. The community as a whole is becoming economically depressed. Crime is up, including burglaries and domestic abuse. School children are showing signs of stress that include falling grades and physical confrontations. Parties on both sides have raised good arguments for not meeting each others' demands. You are not a member of the union, but lost your job two months into the strike because it relied on the business of the company tied up in the strike. In addition to what is becoming major debt, you and your spouse have been told that adoption proceedings will have to be put on hold until your economic situation improves. The company is hiring replacement workers, and you are thinking of crossing the picket lines. What reasons are there for doing so? For not doing so?

■ A heart is available for transplant and is suitable for each of the following patients. To whom should the heart go?

    a. Marta, 12 years old and a musical prodigy
    b. Tomas, 38 years old and a brilliant surgeon

Whistle-blowers

Read aloud and discuss. In discussing the case study, it may stretch thinking to divide into two groups and arbitrarily assign each group one of the positions to argue.

Whistle-blowing is pointing out the wrongdoing or possible dangers of another person's or group's actions.

Below is a case study. Debate the merits of being a whistle-blower in the situation. Include as part of the discussion the effects of either decision on the wider community or the world, whether more information is needed, and how as a Christian one could support a person in this situation.

■ You work in a major research center. The results of current research could save or improve the quality of life for millions of people. The majority of the center's funding comes from donations, but is not enough to sustain the research. You have discovered that a decision has been made to sell research findings to a firm involved in germ warfare. You're thinking of leaking this information to the press. Why would you? Why wouldn't you?

Consider this

Many denominations are engaged in national and global social, economic, and political issues both as a larger church body and through the work of their individual congregations. For most, this involvement is seen as a corporate church witness; it is based on a gospel of love for all.

■ **Under what circumstances do you feel the church—either as a larger body or an individual congregation—should get involved in the business of businesses?**

A further look

Read Luke 9:25.

■ How would you measure whether you were in danger of "losing" yourself in the workplace?

Discovery

Read aloud, then discuss. In doing the rankings, suggest participants line up along an imaginary line between two walls, with one wall being 1 and the other 10. Then have those who cluster on either side and in the middle share why they chose the position they did.

The business of business is business. Whether it's the family farm, a home day care center, the military, a multimillion-dollar corporation, or any of the other thousands of types of businesses, each one makes decisions—consciously or unconsciously—about how that business affects life in the community and world. Using a scale of 1 to 10, with 1 being *not at all responsible* and 10 being *extremely responsible*, share how responsible you feel a business is for:

a. assuring all earn a livable wage.
b. not harming the environment.
c. investing in the community in which it resides.
d. providing safe work environments.
e. providing flexibility of schedules that nurture family life and/or community involvement.

Consider this

PhotoDisc, Inc. © 1995

■ **What scares you most about being unemployed? Why? What part does such fear play in living out one's Christian ethics?**

The world is ours

Much has been written about our responsibility as stewards of God's creation. Genesis 1:26-30 says: "Let us make humankind in our image, according to our likeness; and let them have dominion over the fish . . . the birds . . . the cattle . . . the wild animals . . . and every creeping thing."

■ What do you think it means for humankind to "have dominion" over the rest of creation?

■ How does this concept fit with a discussion or ethics in the workplace? Then, ask for God's guidance in your stewardship role for creation. Record in writing in the appendix what actions you feel led to take.

A further look

Read aloud. Suggest a circle prayer in which members hold hands and each say a sentence or two in prayer.

Read Luke 22:31-34; 54-62.

Peter lacked the moral courage that night in the high priest's courtyard to carry out his resolve to stand by Jesus. We are like Peter in many ways. Though we may not openly deny Jesus, we may deny him in more subtle ways. And there will most certainly be many times when our best efforts to live out our Christian ethics will fall short. As with Peter, however, our failures will not separate us from Christ. Pray now for the courage to live as Christ would have us live and thank God for the grace, mercy, and love that is ours always.

Together in Christ

It is hoped that your participation in this small group has challenged, inspired, and strengthened you for your journey as a faithful Christian in the workplace while making you more aware of how one person's ethical choices can reach beyond the workplace and into the world. We hope, too, that the relationships you have formed will continue and that you will provide ongoing friendship and support for each other.

■ Look back at each session and review the biblical and other models you have discussed for ethical decision-making.

■ Create a plan for how you would go about making a tough ethical decision in your workplace. You may want to make a list of steps you would take (pray, search the Bible, seek advice, and so forth). Or, you may wish to adapt one of the models discussed in the course.

■ Review the section entitled "Integrity" in chapter 1 on page 14. What motto, Bible verse, or thought can help you work toward integrity in living out your Christian ethics in the workplace?

Wrap-up

Before you go, take time for the following:

- Group ministry task

- Review

- Personal concerns and prayer concerns

- Closing prayers

Daily walk

Bible readings

Day 1
John 3:17-21

Day 2
Romans 12:3-8

Day 3
Ephesians 4:25-32

Day 4
Philippians 2:3-11

Day 5
2 Corinthians 6:14-18

Day 6
James 3:13-18

Day 7
Proverbs 20:5-7

Verse for the journey

"Let each of you lead the life that the Lord has assigned, to which God called you" (1 Corinthians 7:17).

Thought for the journey

Always, in some way, another person's journey is affected by the path I walk.

Prayer for the journey

Dear Lord, forgive us when we fail to live our Christian faith with integrity and grant us the wisdom, care, and strength to continue on the journey. Amen

Appendix

Record information about group members here.

Names   **Addresses**   **Phone numbers**

_____

_____

_____

_____

_____

_____

_____

_____

_____

_____

Group commitments

Do not be conformed to this world, but be transformed by the renewing of your minds, so that you may discern what is the will of God—what is good and acceptable and perfect. Romans 12:2

- For our time together, we have made the following commitments to each other

- Goals for our study of this topic are

- Our group ministry task is

- My personal action plan is

Prayer requests

Prayers

■ Closing Prayer

Lord God, you have called your servants
to ventures of which we cannot see the
ending, by paths as yet untrodden,
through perils unknown. Give us faith to
go out with good courage, not knowing
where we go, but only that your hand is
leading us and your love supporting us;
through Jesus Christ our Lord. Amen

Lutheran Book of Worship, © 1978, page 153

■ The Lord's Prayer

(If you plan to pray the Lord's Prayer, record the
version your group uses in the next column.)

Resources

Blanchard, Kenneth and Norman Vincent
Peale. *The Power of Ethical Management*.
New York: William Morrow Company,
1988.

Childs, James M. Jr. *Ethics in Business, Faith
at Work*. Minneapolis: Augsburg Fortress,
1995.

Covey, Stephen R. *Principle-centered Leadership*. New York: Summit Books, 1991.

Forell, George Wolfgang. *The Christian
Lifestyle*. Minneapolis: Augsburg Fortress,
1975.

Gilley, Kay. *Leading from the Heart: Choosing
Courage over Fear in the Workplace*. Newton,
Mass.: Butterworth Heinemann, 1997.

Jones, Laurie Beth. *Jesus, CEO: Using An-
cient Wisdom for Visionary Leadership*. New
York: Hyperion, 1994.

Menninger, Karl M.D. *Whatever Became of
Sin*. New York: Hawthorn Books, 1976.

Rasmussen, Larry. *Earth Community, Earth
Ethics*. Maryknoll, N.Y.: Orbis: 1996.

Rasmussen, Larry. *Moral Fragments and
Moral Community*. Minneapolis: Fortress
Press, 1993.

Stringfellow, William. *An Ethic for Christians and other Aliens in a Strange Land*.
Waco, Texas: Word Books, 1973.

Wuthnow, Robert S. *The Crisis in the
Churches*. New York: Oxford University
Press, 1997.

Name _____

Address _____

_____

Daytime telephone _____

Please check the INTERSECTIONS book you are evaluating.

☐ The Bible and Life   ☐ Following Jesus   ☐ Peace

☐ Captive and Free   ☐ Integrity   ☐ Praying

☐ Caring and Community   ☐ Jesus: Divine and Human   ☐ Reconcilable Differences

☐ Death and Grief   ☐ Managing Stress   ☐ Self-Esteem

☐ Divorce   ☐ Men and Women   ☐ Smart Choices

☐ Faith   ☐ Parenting

Please tell us about your small group.

1. Our group had an average attendance of _____.

2. Our group was made up of
   ___ Young adults (19-25 years).
   ___ Adults (most between 25-45 years).
   ___ Adults (most between 45-60 years).
   ___ Adults (most between 60-75 years).
   ___ Adults (most 75 and over).
   ___ Adults (wide mix of ages).
   ___ Men (number) and ___ women (number).

3. Our group (answer as many as apply)
   ___ came together for the sole purpose of studying this INTERSECTIONS book.
   ___ has decided to study another INTERSECTIONS book.
   ___ is an ongoing Sunday school group.
   ___ met at a time other than Sunday morning.
   ___ had only one facilitator for this study.

Please tell us about your experience with INTERSECTIONS.

4. What I like best about my INTERSECTIONS experience is

5. Three things I want to see the same in future INTERSECTIONS books are

6. Three things I might change in future INTERSECTIONS books are

7. Topics I would like developed for new INTERSECTIONS books are

8. Our group had ___ sessions for the six chapters of this book.

9. Other comments I have about INTERSECTIONS are

_____

Thank you for taking the time to fill out and return this questionnaire.

FOLD CARD IN HERE, SEAL WITH TAPE, AND MAIL TODAY!

BUSINESS REPLY MAIL

FIRST-CLASS MAIL   PERMIT NO. 22120   MINNEAPOLIS, MN

POSTAGE WILL BE PAID BY ADDRESSEE

Augsburg Fortress

ATTN INTERSECTIONS TEAM
PO BOX 1209
MINNEAPOLIS MN 55440-8807